Weird, wild, and wonderful Worms

By Rose Inserra

Gareth Stevens
Publishing

Please visit our Web site **www.garethstevens.com**. For a free color catalog of all our high-quality books, call toll free 1-800-542-2595 or fax 1-877-542-2596.

Library of Congress Cataloging-in-Publication Data

Inserra, Rose, 1958-
Worms / Rose Inserra.
    p. cm. — (Weird, wild, and wonderful)
Includes index.
ISBN 978-1-4339-3577-0 (library binding)
1. Worms—Juvenile literature. I. Title.
QL386.6.I57 2010
592'.3—dc22

2009043883

Published in 2010 by
Gareth Stevens Publishing
111 East 14th Street, Suite 349
New York, NY 10003

For Gareth Stevens Publishing:
Art Direction: Haley Harasymiw
Editorial Direction: Kerri O'Donnell

Designed in Australia by www.design-ed.com.au

Photography by Kathie Atkinson
Additional photographs: © Newspix / News Ltd, p. 10a; Alan Henderson, reproduced courtesy of Museum Victoria, p. 10b; Ralph and Daphne Keller/ANTPhoto.com, p. 11.

Printed in the United States of America

CPSIA compliance information: Batch #CW10GS: For further information contact Gareth Stevens, New York, New York, at 1-800-542-2595.

Contents

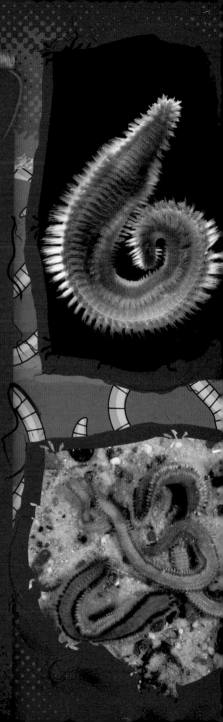

What Are Worms?

Worms are **invertebrates**. That means they have no backbone. Some worms have no eyes or teeth and are smooth. Others have long **bristles** (small hairs) and **tentacles**. Some have jaws and are **carnivores**.

Worms are **annelids**. All annelids have long, round bodies made up of **segments**. Their heads and tails look the same.

The earthworm is the most common annelid. It does not have eyes, nose, or ears. Instead, it has **sensors** on its body. These sense movement and light.

4

There are three groups of annelids.

1. Earthworms

These worms can be found in soil everywhere. They can be used to make a wonderful, healthy garden. They can also be used as fishing bait.

2. Marine worms

You find **marine** worms at the beach and in the sea. They have long bristles. This helps them move around on rocks. Some look like weird plants.

3. Leeches

Leeches can live on land and in water. They have sharp teeth and strong suckers. The teeth cut into a person's or animal's skin. Then, with their strong suckers, they suck blood from the cut. Wild!

Tube worms have lots of feeding tentacles. They hide in their tubes when they are scared.

This marine worm looks like spaghetti. It hides under rocks and in rock pools. Its tentacles come out to pick up bits of seaweed to eat.

Nightcrawlers

There are about 3,000 types of earthworms. Garden earthworms have soft bodies. They are mostly brown and pink. You find them in the garden and under stones and logs.

Earthworms breathe through their skin. Their skin has to stay wet so the air can get through. Earthworms love dark, moist places in the ground.

Fact Bite

Earthworms are eaten by snakes, toads, birds, foxes, beetles, flatworms, and leeches.

Earthworms are called "nightcrawlers." This is because they come out at night to feed.

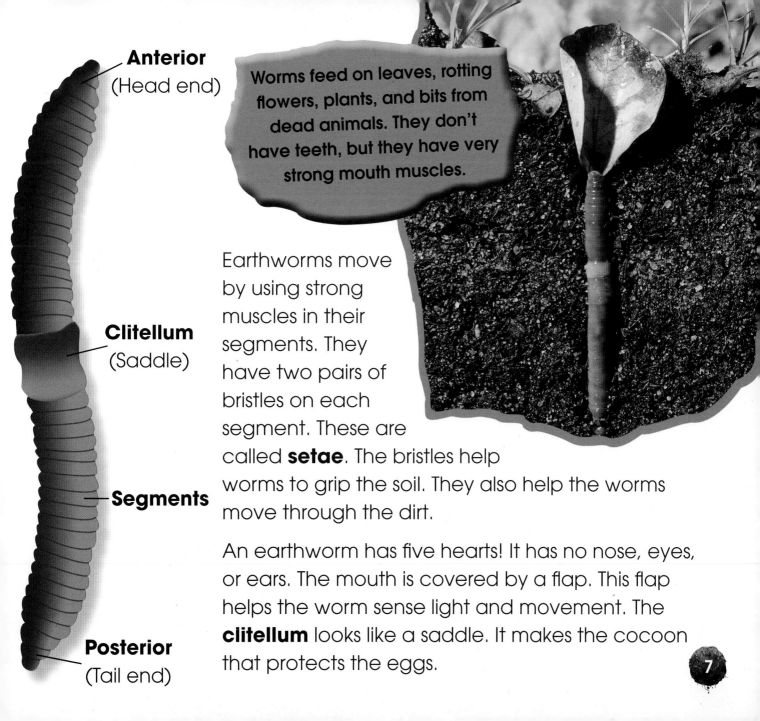

Anterior
(Head end)

Clitellum
(Saddle)

Segments

Posterior
(Tail end)

Worms feed on leaves, rotting flowers, plants, and bits from dead animals. They don't have teeth, but they have very strong mouth muscles.

Earthworms move by using strong muscles in their segments. They have two pairs of bristles on each segment. These are called **setae**. The bristles help worms to grip the soil. They also help the worms move through the dirt.

An earthworm has five hearts! It has no nose, eyes, or ears. The mouth is covered by a flap. This flap helps the worm sense light and movement. The **clitellum** looks like a saddle. It makes the cocoon that protects the eggs.

Hungry Waste Eaters

Worms are great for gardens. Lots of worms mean healthy soil.

Earthworms help keep soil loose and airy. They turn over the soil when they move through it. That makes it easy for **nutrients** and water to soak into the soil. Worms are like wild gardeners!

After they come out to feed, they leave their droppings (**casts**). Casts make the soil rich and healthy. Plants and vegetables grow bigger and faster.

Worm casts look like round swirls of mud.

There are three types of **compost** earthworms: tiger worms, red wrigglers, and Indian blues. A compost worm farm is a wonderful way to **recycle** waste.

These striped worms are called tiger worms.

Make a Compost Worm Farm

You will need:
- 2 **polystyrene** boxes with lids
- an insect screen
- damp, shredded newspaper
- food scraps
- water
- garden soil
- 1,000 worms

How to make the compost worm farm:
1. Make holes in the lid and the bottom of the first box.
2. Spread the insect screen on the bottom (over the holes).
3. Fill the box with damp, shredded newspaper and garden soil.
4. Add the worms.
5. Place the first box over the second box. This is so the water can drain. Put a lid on the first box.
6. Add food scraps.
7. Keep the boxes in a cool spot. When there's lots of casts and liquid, empty the second box and put it in your garden.

Underground Giants

The giant Gippsland earthworm is the world's largest earthworm. When it is stretched, it can be $6\frac{1}{2}$ feet (2 m) long. That's the size of a tall person.

The giant Gippsland worm is only found in a small area in Gippsland, Victoria, in Australia. It was discovered about 100 years ago. It has a pink and grey body with a purple head.

A farmer holding up a giant earthworm

There are fewer giant Gippsland worms each year. Farmers cut down trees to clear land so they can graze cattle. Fewer trees means less food for the worms. Cattle are also a threat to the worms. They trample on them if they come up.

Farmers use toxic sprays on their land to kill bugs and weeds. The worms eat or soak up the poison through their skin. This kills them.

The giant Gippsland worm is protected. That means people are not allowed to harm them. Their bodies are very soft. They bruise easily. They die if they are dug out of their burrows.

It takes 12 months for the worm to **hatch** from an egg. It takes 5 years for the young worm to become an adult.

These giant worms spend most of the time underground. They like to live in deep, moist burrows near creeks and water springs.

Marine Worms

Scale worms hunt small sea creatures.

Marine worms live in many places around water. Some hang on to the bodies of other water animals. Others swim in the ocean. Some worms burrow into the sand or mud. Some build tubes underwater.

Marine worms come in many shapes and sizes. They can look like fans, coral, or plants. They have long bristles and flaps down their bodies. This helps them to swim, burrow, and catch bits of food.

The sand worm is big. It hides under rocks or in burrows in shallow water.

12

Some marine worms have wonderful colored tentacles. They use them to stir up sand and grab food as it floats past.

Fire worms are carnivores. They hunt for their food. They have eyes, tentacles, and a mouth with jaws. The side flaps have poisonous bristles. This helps protect them from **predators**.

Fire worms have long bristles as sharp as needles. They cause a hot, burning pain if you touch them. That is why they are called "fire" worms. Ouch!

Fact bite

Marine worms are called *polychaetes*. That means "many bristles."

These small, slender worms are found on the Great Barrier Reef, Australia.

Hiding on the Beach

Giant beach worms burrow in wet, sandy areas on the beach.

This man is trying to catch a beach worm. He dangles some fish on the end of the line. The worm will poke its head up to eat the fish. Then the man will grab the worm!

Next time you go to the beach, watch out for giant beach worms. They live in burrows under the wet sand. They hide away from predators—and humans. That's because people use giant beach worms as fishing bait.

At the beach are thousands of tiny tube worms. You can see them on rocks and in rock pools. They look like weird shells.

Tube worms don't ever leave their tubes. They just stick out their tentacles. They use their tentacles to catch food.

While the tide is out, the worms close off their tubes. They have a little cap they can close. This keeps them safe from predators and the weather. When the tide comes back in, they open the cap. The tentacles come out again, looking for food.

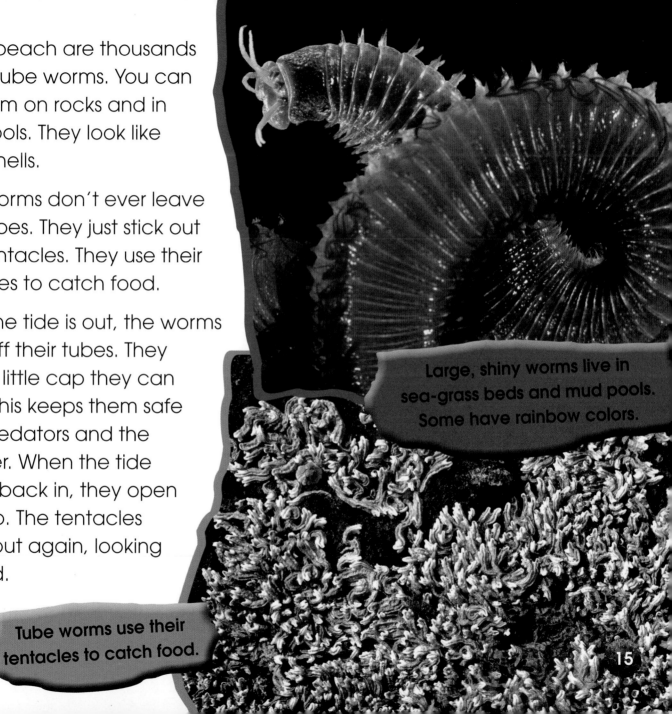

Large, shiny worms live in sea-grass beds and mud pools. Some have rainbow colors.

Tube worms use their tentacles to catch food.

Worms in a Tube

Tube worms live in tubes. They build them from bits of coral, shells, and seaweed. The tubes are tough. Predators can't bite through them. Only the worm's feeding tentacles stick out from its tube. The tentacles catch food as it floats by.

Christmas tree tube worms live on the Great Barrier Reef, Australia. They have spirals in many colors.

These fan worms look like they belong in a garden. Only their feathery tentacles can be seen.

The fan worm's tentacles look like flowers.

Tube worms have bristles that are shaped like hooks. This helps them grip sand or rocks so they can't float out of their tubes. If they don't hide in their tubes, fish and crabs will eat them.

There are many types of tube worms. Some live on the ocean floor and look like flowers. Others are shaped like fans or feather dusters. Some even look like Christmas trees!

This worm is out of its tube. If it's not careful, a fish might eat it!

A Slimy New Life

Earthworms and some marine worms are **hermaphrodites**. That means they are both a male and a female. However, it takes two of them to produce their young.

Earthworms mate when the ground is wet after rain. Most worms come out of their burrows to find a mate. However, some look for a mate in a burrow underground.

Earthworms lay their eggs in soil. The eggs are in little cocoons.

The cocoon is very soft at first. After a while, it hardens. This protects the eggs inside.

During mating, the bump in the middle of the worm makes a kind of slime. After mating, the slime forms tiny cocoons. The cocoons slide off the worms. Inside the cocoons are worm eggs.

The eggs turn into baby worms. They grow until they hatch from their cocoons. This can take from three weeks to five months. They can now wriggle on their own and look for food.

Marine worms don't have cocoons. Most shed their eggs into the sea. The baby worms hatch in the sea. Then they swim away.

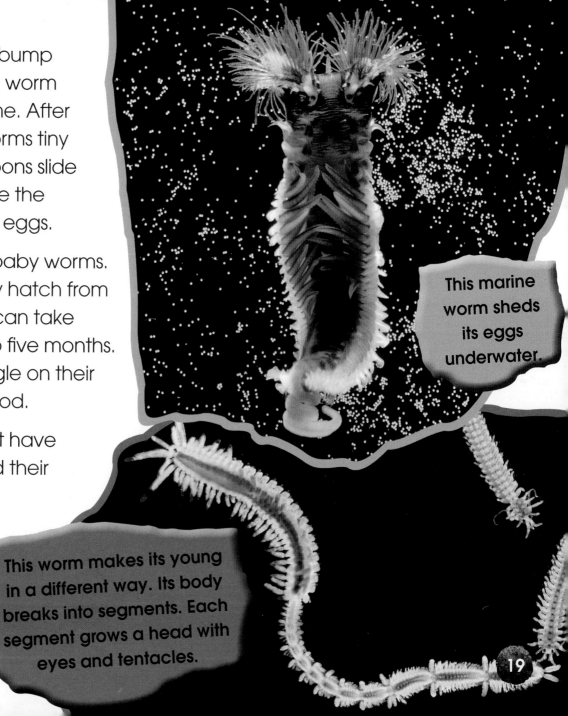

This marine worm sheds its eggs underwater.

This worm makes its young in a different way. Its body breaks into segments. Each segment grows a head with eyes and tentacles.

Growing Pains

The worm's soft body can get hurt easily. If a body part is broken, the worm can grow new parts. Some even grow new worms from their broken body parts.

Fish eat fat, juicy worms. This worm escaped, but without its head. It's lucky it can grow a new one!

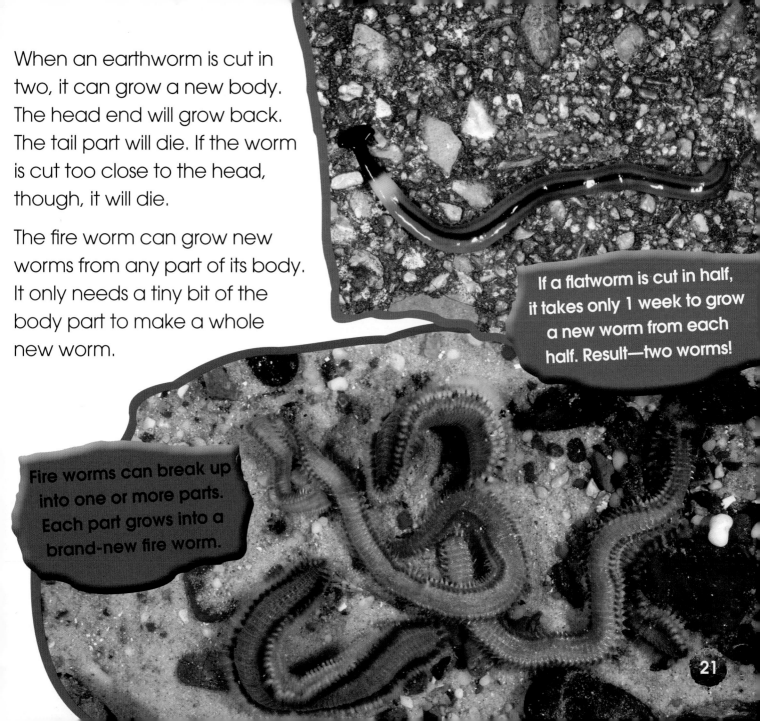

When an earthworm is cut in two, it can grow a new body. The head end will grow back. The tail part will die. If the worm is cut too close to the head, though, it will die.

The fire worm can grow new worms from any part of its body. It only needs a tiny bit of the body part to make a whole new worm.

If a flatworm is cut in half, it takes only 1 week to grow a new worm from each half. Result—two worms!

Fire worms can break up into one or more parts. Each part grows into a brand-new fire worm.

Fact File: Worm Characteristics

Worms are made up of three groups: earthworms, marine worms, and leeches. They live in many habitats—land, oceans, and freshwater rivers and lakes.

Worm Characteristics		
Earthworms	**Marine worms**	**Leeches**
• live in dirt • burrow	• live in the sea or on the beach • burrow, hide in tubes, or float	• live near water
• body segments • short bristles • have sensors to feel movement • blind	• have many bristles • have tentacles or flaps	• have a front sucker and a back sucker • have sharp teeth
• eat rotting plants and animals	• eat all ocean foods	• suck blood for food
• hermaphrodites	• some hermaphrodites	• hermaphrodites
• can grow new parts	• can grow new parts	

Glossary

annelids — worms that have bodies made up of segments

bristles — small hairs

burrow — a hole in the ground made by animals

carnivores — animals that eat meat

casts — worm droppings

clitellum — the swollen bump in the middle of an earthworm

compost — dead plants and kitchen waste mixed and left to rot

hatch — when a baby worm comes out of its cocoon

hermaphrodite — being both a male and a female

invertebrates — animals with no backbone

marine — belonging to the ocean

nutrients — goodness for plants and vegetables to grow

polystyrene — a type of soft, foamy plastic

predators — animals that hunt other animals for food

recycle — something that can be used again

segments — small parts

sensors — special parts of the animal for sensing movement and light

setae — two pairs of bristles under each segment

tentacles — long, thin growths on the head or near the mouth of some animals

For Further Information

Books

French, Vivian. *Yucky Worms*. Somerville, MA: Candlewick Press, 2010.

Tocci, Salvatore. *Marine Habitats: Life in Saltwater*. New York: Scholastic, Inc., 2004.

Web Sites

All About Earthworms
http://yucky.discovery.com/flash/worm/pg000102.html

Sea Worms
http://www.seasky.org/reeflife/sea2c.html

Publisher's note to educators and parents: Our editors have carefully reviewed these Web sites to ensure that they are suitable for students. Many Web sites change frequently, however, and we cannot guarantee that a site's future contents will continue to meet our high standards of quality and educational value. Be advised that students should be closely supervised whenever they access the Internet.

Index